We Carry the Cave

Bill Jenkins

We Carry the Cave

For my wife, Heather,
our children,
Alex, Hugo and Cleo,
and our grandchildren,
lsabella, lsaac,
Wolfgang and Stirling

We Carry the Cave
ISBN 978 1 76041 611 9
Copyright © text Bill Jenkins 2018
Cover photo: Campfire – Stirling Ranges National Park, by Jesse

First published 2018 by
Ginninderra Press
PO Box 3461 Port Adelaide 5015 Australia
www.ginninderrapress.com.au

Contents

Preface	7
On a day like any other…	9
The Road to Nowhere	11
The Agèd Jihadi	12
Everywhere Mountains	14
Dull Fire	15
Fear	16
All of Us	17
Positive Poison	18
The Hospice Snake	19
End of Day	20
Feed my Fire	21
The Death of Decency	22
Empty Souls	23
The Serpent – After Eden	24
Election Again	25
Pruning the Bonsai	26
We Carry the Cave	27
A Wet Night	28
The Path	29
Original Sin?	30
A Clear Fog	31
Goodbye Grief	32
Breath	33
Babel	34
Crow	35
The Dismal Chorus	36
Battles	37
Home	39
Scars	40

The Box Tree	41
Our Cortex	42
Thunder	43
Books at Home	44
I am the poem	45
We are the Poem	46
Take It All Away	47
Trivia	48
Just a Thought	49
Every Life	50
How it Begins	51
Just Not Seen	52
Darkness	53
Ambitions	54
The Apricot Leaf	55
In the Beginning	56
Our Words	57
Letting Go	58
The Young Jihadi	59
What we Know?	61
There's Always One	62
The Pallid Stream	63
Your Path	64
It Can Only Be Said	65
In Ancient Times	66
Shedding	67
Storm	68
Not Living	69
Dawdling Down the Street	70
On Death in the Orchard	71
For God's Sake!	72

Preface

Recently, while giving a talk at the Melbourne Savage Club, the question 'Does poetry matter?' was raised. This book concerns one reason why poetry matters, in a personal sense.

Like other human activities – such as art, sculpture, writing, sport, dance, gardening and so on – poetry is an expression of the self. We reveal who we are through what we do, what we produce. Some activities are of course more revealing than others! It is also true that some poetry is more revealing than other poetry.

My poetry is very personal; it is driven by and reflects my interests and my personal experience. It is a vehicle for my identity and provides an indirect, yet discernible self portrait.

When I was about three years old, my Scottish maternal grandfather, James Walker Ritchie, died. All I can remember of him is the smell of whisky and the sharp sizzle sound as a gob of spit hit the open fire. Apart from the fact that he was a builder, a carpenter, and that he made Ramsay MacDonald's coffin and led the funeral cortège from the kirk down to Spynie Cemetery, I know nothing at all about the man, the person that he was. As I got older, I came to wish that I had known him better.

I don't spit in the fire, but I do drink whisky. I would like my grandchildren, if they want to, as they get older, to be able to know more of me if they wish, what kind of a man I was. Reading these poems will help.

On a day like any other…

On a day like any other,
they both wait like beetles
in the dark,
for the light,
so that scuttling, they can
seek the dark, to wait again.

She would welcome death – his!
And so would he.
Instead he milks her breast of scorn
and wants his pillow fluffed,
dark stained and damp
with ancient tears.

On a day like any other,
she bellows broad
the aching of their days,
charging strangers dear
with uttered pain for sympathy.

No friend in this small house,
none, not one to see
the apparatus of a dying man,
hid well in drawers
and capsuled dreams.

On a day like any other,
he lies unfinished,
a cankered doll, limp
and lost, discarded,
but for she who tears his ears
and pokes his eyes
seeking his mortality.

On a day like any other…

The Road to Nowhere

As you look about, you see spaces
Not completion, not perfection
You see too that things are broken
But that's OK!
You can live in a land like this
Since nothing is ever right
Until death wipes the trial
That is you
Off the face of the earth.
Then you will be complete
As perfect as you will ever be.
From perfection to perfection
From completeness to complete
By a stumbling kind of way,
The road we all share,
The road to nowhere.

The Agèd Jihadi

If you could see his world
you would be smoothly shocked.
If you could hear his world
you could gather the absent voices
disembodied, unconnected, ranting,
God riven diatribes and bluster.

If you could see his self,
his smiles, his depthless eyes,
you would be stunned by the dullness.
Behind the ageing veiled façade
spectred, dark and smoky shadows,
lurk behind his black and banded gaze.

If you could feel his heart,
his warmth, his arms, his love,
you would feel little less
than if you had felt nothing.
You might however feel a pounding tremble,
the debris of a life of fear.

If you could taste his world,
wine would seem bizarre,
putrid with a gangrenous aftertaste,
lingering long on the back of the palate.
While you might prefer notes of berry fruit,
these would be dank and discordant.

If you could smell his world,
orange blossom would reek,
wisteria would dim your mind,
while bitter honeysuckle would be recalled
until the day you died,
as an acrid air, a friably faecal fusion.

If you could know his world,
you would relish relentless death,
apprehend the ways of friendless days,
the inherent imbecility of darkness,
the chaos of his life's achievements,
and a fractured and fragmented soul

Everywhere Mountains

Can we breech
The truth of mountains?
Can we pass the prone
And petrified,
Defiantly passive aggressive,
Standing in every way?
Some can find a narrow cleft,
A squeeze
Some can pass like a bird
On a breeze,
Through patchy snow
Or broken cloud.
But most need hammer
And chisel,
Infinite time and focus,
To chip through
The rock, the solid rock
Of mountains.

Dull Fire

Smoke drifts across the roof,
no direction,
wafts like a dream,
wanders from the flue.

Below a fire must burn,
dull and damp,
a feeble fire,
not a bone burner.

I can feel this fire,
neither rabid nor wistful,
just drivelling along,
barely warm.

No soul blaze,
no danger,
no fear of sparks spitting,
no fervour to quench,

just dull fire…

Fear

It's so hard to avoid
Facing the fear
When it leaps out
And grips your gut.
So face to face,
What do you say?
What do you do?
Most of the time nothing,
Except lose your grip
On bladder and bowel,
And gain the skill to utter
Blatant gibberish.

All of Us

'…any man's death diminishes me, because I am involved in
mankind, and therefore never send to know for whom the bell tolls;
It tolls for thee…' John Donne, *Meditation XVII*

All of us are between knife and throat,
We are in the ruins of Aleppo, all of us,
We are victims and murderers, all of us.
We share blood with every human child,
We are found in every violent family,
Hearing the screams, chilling screams
Echo in every home with bleeding children.
We are before and behind every blow, all of us,
Thrown through the anger we share, and use.
We are, all of us, on the drunken streets
Where fists and knives are the order of the day,
We hold them, we feel them sharp, hard,
We feel the thrust, the piercing agony,
And we feel the darkness, all of us.
Behind our backs we shut our eyes, all of us,
Thoughtless, mindless, conscience blind
To participation through the life we share,
It's not us and them, it's all of us.

Positive Poison

We need a poem,
to speak for all
who feel alienated by the culture
of the positive,
by this culture of the hollow and false.

Let it come!
Let the acidic avalanche
Stream from above,
Carving its path
Ingenuously
through the soft stone of our lives.

The bloat is felt,
inflated by lies;
how grateful we are,
some, like Oliver Twist
Say 'More, please.'
Keep us safely ill-informed,
please, they beg.

Positive lies,
the poisonous stultifiers of life,
are smoothed across our geography
like buttered arsenic on toast,
nourishing and destroying ad infinitum.

The Hospice Snake

A normal kind of a day
as they go in the hospice
when a snake
seemed to have gained access,
without referral.

The dugite, as it was, gave rise
to excited discussion
with two possibilities.
The first was that the snake
had triggered the automatic doors;
the second, that it had come in
on someone's heels.
But there was a third,
which was not raised,
that it belonged in the place,
that it was a creature of the hospice,
a manifestation of the darker side
of the compassion
which was the foundation
and the nourishment of the place,
an elusive but essential marker
of the unimaginable cost of love,
life and time.

End of Day

Birds have disappeared
But not their sounds
So too the bees are gone
The air is light
Satisfying and full
A bit like a postcard
Hover flies have gone
The sunlight is heavy
Maybe it's the time
Though maybe not
The pictures still hang
The dogs remain at rest
No butterflies in sight
Calm has returned
Not a hint of chaos
Bird calls eerily frantic
Aggressive and close
We are still warm
The two dogs and I
Poetry is a tad heavier
But still the books lean
Coffee replaced by wine
Dinner satisfies just
Quiet reappears
The bed stays unmade.

Feed my Fire

Feed my fire, dearest
Set another log
On the embers.
Keep my fire alive,
Never mind the smoke
As is said by many
Where there's smoke
Then with a bit of a blow
On the weakest ember
We might hope for a blaze.

The Death of Decency

Decency, it's time to hide.
There will be a civil war,
But it will not be civil.
You will lose, no doubt.
You have no weapons.
'You are an immoral twerp.'
Or 'Go away you racist!'
Will not overwhelm fascists
Whose armoury is deep
With pockets much deeper
Who will first destroy the world
Verbally, 'You dog! You little dog!'
Only fascists will get bank loans,
And then the very very special,
Will get free iPhones.
Hide, decency, hide, no place for you
In this damned world,
Where the most fragile
And angriest of the human race,
Driven by the engines of insecurity,
Puerile defensive fear,
O, and blind unadulterated hatred,
Will rise up and scoff, in groups,
Pissing on the shroud of religion
Shitting on the birth of humanism,
Where even the appearance of nicety
Will be seen to be pathetic.
Decency, you have had your day,
If ever a day you had!

Empty Souls

'All empty souls tend to extreme opinion. It is only those who have built up a rich world of memories and habits of thought that extreme opinions affront the sense of probability.' – W.B. Yeats

Can you feel the rattle?
Can you hear the cold?
Is your soul empty?
Is your soul bold?
It could be immaterial.
Hell, it is immaterial,
If it's anything at all.

It needs no space,
But it must be filled,
It must be tilled,
Worked like the soil,
To nullify extremities.

The Serpent – After Eden

After Eden, job well done, the serpent
went on from sex, knowledge
and temptation
to lesser and greater things.
On his adventures,
he spent some time as a scorpion,
as big as a chicken,
dealing death
on the dusty roads
and villages in India.
Easy to see
but difficult to escape.
His greatest achievement
was when, as a water buffalo,
he offered to carry a whole village
to safety from the ravages of floods
only to sink slowly
beneath the raging waters
when they all thought
they were safe on his back:
a silent and submersible antithesis
to the sainted Christophorus.
Later, as a human being, a holy man,
he helped form some relationships
of warmth and trust between adolescents
only to create murder through betrayal.
This he enjoyed immensely;
much more than the banality of temptation.

Election Again

It's that time again!
Can you feel the lead in the air?
Every breath burdened by promises
that will never be kept.
Every ballooning and mockingly sincere lie
floating aimlessly away untouched, unfelt
waiting to be popped
by any four year old.

Who wants to avoid this slanderous fog,
with vague performers mouthing
assertively obscure lines?
Who wants to breathe clean unfoetid air?
Who would actually choose to be amused by besuited jokers?
Who?

But let me say before you say,
since it's been said and said and said before:
maybe we deserve it.
Maybe we don't want sincerity, intelligence and truth.
Maybe we prefer the jokers to the real.
Maybe we prefer balloons and blown up paper bags,
so that with a pin and a prick
we can at least get a bang out of it all.

Pruning the Bonsai

A pure act of faith
Stripping the bonsai
Back to its twisted torso
Discarding all leaves
Leaving naked stumps
Hope carried blind
On prospective acts
Survival and regrowth
Again, again, and again
Through another pruning.

We Carry the Cave

We carry the cave
From the start
Alone and together.
We carry the dark
We carry the shadows,
The sun dying at the door
The warmth turning cold
Bringing us together.
We carry the fire
Its lambent light
Making images
Dance on the walls,
Gifting us, feeding us,
Taking us beyond.
From the cave
We carry our past
And seek our future,
Trusting only the visions
We carry from the flames.

A Wet Night

Rain through the night
A dry but still dawn
Not a breeze
Lingering drips fall
From the leaf filled gutter
Leaves drop from trees straight
Not much tumbling
Possums mostly mumbling
With the occasional shriek
Insects hiding in holes
Clouds now thinning
Sunlight's volume's up
Birds begin to chatter
And then the rain again
Another symphony
On the old tin roof.

The Path

There are no signs
For us to follow
In the wilderness,
Through the mist.

We make a path
By putting
One foot before another,
Often at ease
Sometimes not.

It is unique this path
With a discernible direction
And a finite end.

Then the wind blows
The footprints fade
Filling with dust
And the path?
It disappears
Like all paths.

Original Sin?

Take a snake called Temptation,
An apple, with a touch of knowledge,
A more than luscious garden,
Two nudes with coincident genitalia,
A pinch of disobedience,
And there you have it,
The recipe for…original sin,
The stuff upon which our culture feeds,
The sin that separates us from God.

So we want sex, knowledge and freedom,
More than we want God. Who wouldn't?

So why didn't God choose a better sin,
A bigger sin, for the original?
One of the ten on the tablets maybe?
He could have chosen 'Thou shall not kill.'
He could have got a father…
With a very sharp knife,
A captive life with a neck, kneeling,
And a young son with large eyes,
Who hardly had the strength
To hold the head,
That he was given by his dad.
Now that's an original sin,
More to feed on,
Badness beyond belief.

And He wouldn't need a garden,
Any old desert would do,
With any old TV crew.

A Clear Fog

It neither rises nor descends
This clear fog.
It is carried by thought
Upon thought, upon thought,
A train ever growing until
It fills the mind
Clearly coagulated
Every lens amiss
open to the world
Astigmatic, colour blind
Biased towards
The dismal and despairing
Changed only by drops
By single drops of colour
Each drop part lens correction
Until one can see again, patchy,
Unstuck, freely, fully,
The world mirrored in colour
The colour of the world.

Goodbye Grief

It's time, as they say
To let the grief go
It's not as if it has warmed
You or kept you safe
Or been a pleasant surprise
It has just been a substitute
A poor one at that for loss
And the emptiness it carries
Throughout our life
As we struggle to live
Without the one who's gone
As we search for the new
A poor substitute for life
And nothing like the joy
That brought us grief
In the first place.

Breath

Breath is a meeting of life
Between the air and us.
We gain much
Our life is sustained.
A gifted meeting, divine
It might be said,
Singing the living tempo,
For the dance of our life.

Babel

God kept his side of the bargain
but the rest reneged,
and talked to each other about themselves,
threw in the towel
and built a tower called Babel
using their needs as bricks
and their promises
as mortar.

What a tower!

'Let's poke a hole in heaven.'
They said in one or more words,
each ego a brick, with more than
ample ambition to hold them together.

God perused this mammoth of word and lie,
each storey a tale
told in a tongue
that licked them together,

and laughed himself into oblivion.

Crow

In that dark cave
where no one has a way
a nest is found
where death lies mute.

As a crow embalmed
fear sits in our hearts
cawing the veils of dark
and despair.

We dive in Montaigne
and find these fears.
We lift them up, polish them
and set them up as ideals.

Happiness, the greatest fear of all
is polished until it gleams
so bright that we see ourself
blinded by our hopes and dreams.

And the cave stays dark
always the nest remains
each sound made
carries echoes for eternity.

The Dismal Chorus

The dismal chorus of morning crows
Seems content to caw away the dark,
Each of the group casting caws
At each other,
Then as if by magic,
Coordinated caws
Smother the greenery, dull weight,
Sitting heavy on the dawn.

Battles

The past is littered with battles,
Mostly bloody, a sure fire mix
For culling the poor and idealistic
And heaping glorious bullshit on the backs
The rubber clad backs of nobility,
Those who are born to rule, they think,
And where fame, with all its elasticity,
Sticks rubber to rubber. They like that.

Waterloo, there's a name,
Remembered for a day or two
Then surrounded by laurels,
Raised in glory by a degree or two
And shot off into the future,
Where it is received more than warmly
By romantics and those addicted
To nostalgia.

Battles aren't like this any more.
They are never named for lack of honour.
They are never warmly received,
The laurel leaves dry and shrivel up
Before you can wink and wind the engines.
They are never remembered in the vastness
Of the murderous rampage,
Substance of our rampant news cycle.

So we glorify the battles of the past
Listed and named in our museums,
Studied by the military, just in case
Honour returns and gentlemen are recreated,
To ensure a battle is suitable for the club,
That it can pay its fees and bar bills faithfully,
So that the quixotic politicians can
Remain mindlessly blind to the costs of war.

Home

Home is a coloured place
Coloured with memories
Of warmth, of anger, of love
And things.
As a place it has its place,
But it is a place plus.
Plus what?
Life!
Life colours the walls,
Whitens the ceilings,
Softens the flooring,
And makes the place breathe.
Home welcomes you,
Supports you,
Gives you purpose
And power enough
To trust yourself
As it is launching pad
And a haven for retreat.
It is the ground beneath your feet,
And the shelter for your heart.

Scars

Nose, neck, hand
Hip, face, feet
Scar sites
Signs of past
Encounters with sharp
Skin being sliced
Regrowth marked
Challenges met
Vivid memories
Drenched in blood.
Then there are scars
Just mindfully visible
Bloodless events
Rejection
Malice
Duplicity
Not one drop of blood
Just oceans of pain.

The Box Tree

The sun shines
between the leaves of the ficus,
the box tree, not so generous,
has other leafy virtues.
The light and sweet sound
of the breeze
through the leaves,
leaves nothing to be desired.
The gentle motion
of these leaves
creates shadows
that could easily become
breathless song.
The breath and the sounding leaves
both speak to me.
And in wilder times,
heavy rain on the leaves makes the Box
dance in time
to the music of thunderous lightning,
from calm order to sweet chaos,
the leaves of the box tree speak
as creation.

Our Cortex

Lying under an abyss of emptiness
The sun seeps through every crevice
Through every closed eyelid.
It is a penetrating insidious force
A weightless back-breaking burden,
Light only in its constant presence
Not going or coming, just staying
With a perfectly balanced stillness
Such as can only be seen not touched
No shade except through reflection
The ever present cortical umbrella
Through which no light intrudes
Creates the meandering fabric
Under which our riotous experience
With all its noise, and turbulence
Can be totally encapsulated.

Thunder

Thunder is an old man
Growling about now,
A warm low sound,
The earth speaking
Through the sky,
Comforting.
A universal grumbling
Touching, often pitiful,
Lasting softly,
Long and low,
Tracing the distance
With streaks of light,
Best when moving away,
Far away.
Worst when up close and personal!

Books at Home

If the floorboards move, they creak;
and dust mites sit in judgement.
But over the fireplace, the mantel
shows no movement, life or fire,
only book upon book upon book.

Each book a burdened burden,
a weight, known and unknown,
speculation, love and beauty
bursting to tell, and even yell
at a deafened incurious world.

The mantel is but one shelf
for a thousand, thousand books,
life's literary curiosities and moments
held together firmly on the outer,
with more fragile ease on the inner.

Books too adorn the floor
on all sides within the rooms;
for vertical shelves with books
terribly functional, a novel façade,
Babylonian gardens dripping life,
paper life fuelled with words
rampant with or without readers,
where truth, truths and lies
are bound firm in a demented mess.

I am the poem

I am the poem
When once a blind river
Raging through the land
Driving all beyond
Across the shallows
Now I am the deepest fjord
Motionless
Reflecting all skies
Disturbed only by mystery
Rising sometime from my depths
Bearing conviction
Breaking my surface
Bringing validity to the world
With nary a ripple
Except if you read me
We become the poem.

We are the Poem

In the box, in the dark
Some of us just sit
Others cry and sob
Many just look at screens
Some demand release,
But we scratch at the walls.
We wonder about the box
How strong is it
The texture of its surface
The dark dimensions
Of this encapsulation
We sit, we stand, we stomp about
How do we feel, we wonder
And those like us, how do they feel
So we find each other
And we ask each other
And so it is
In the box, in the dark
We are the poem.

Take It All Away

Take it all away
The crap, the cares,
The tiredness and stress,
And what is left?
Emptiness?
No, no – you are left
Cleansed!
Vital bones that breathe,
Bear crucial signs,
Life remains,
The priceless remnant.

Trivia

The end will not be natural disaster
Or the annihilation by total war
It will be complete trivialisation
Demolition of meaning
Loss of knowledge of the real
Hope in the unreal
The lordship of fame and celebrity
As if this will save our world
Or make it safe for our young.
What a fucking waste of the true and real.

Just a Thought

And so we are speck upon speck,
We are human in the world,
In the universe,
Infinitesimally small and insignificant.
So what do we do?
We cuddle up to someone
and make them our meaning,
Or we cuddle up to something
and make it what our life revolves around.
What power!
What neediness?
It's absobloodylutely amazing!
He said with touching tmesis!

Every Life

Every laugh is the same laugh
Every cry is the same cry
Every smile is the same smile
Every tear is the same tear
Every love is the same love
Every sorrow is the same sorrow
Every joy is the same joy

Every life is the same life.

How it Begins

In many young
And empty lives
It begins with purpose
As absolute meaning
Turning young quacks
Into destructive ducks
Who will happily kill
And willingly die
On the pavements
Of the world.

Just Not Seen

When all is told
There is much to tell
Open on book shelves
Inside many pages
Between the lines
Not hidden
Just not shown
Just not seen.

Darkness

I like to gaze
wide eyes open
through the window pane
late at night,
till the darkness reflects itself.

If a door bangs
or a floorboard creaks,
it speaks as a bitter start
to a cooler breath of unease,
an heightened sense.

If I look closer at the night,
I can see myself in the dark,
yet in the dark I see nothing,
but for some, in the dark,
everything is seen.

In the dark, when asleep
the moonlight falling
through the window
can dazzle me awake
and leave me wondering.

And at night when a wind
surrounds the house
disrupting a deep sleep,
the darkness remains,
rock solid, undisturbed.

Ambitions

You want to believe
That time remains
For all ambitions
To be achieved,
But you know
We all know
If we think
About this that
A point will be reached
When ambitions decay
Like everything else,
Often before everything else.

The Apricot Leaf

In the orchard
At the end of an apricot branch
A yellowed leaf is touched by the breeze
It trembles but doesn't fall.
What a leaf!

In the Beginning

When did we begin?
With sin?
Hardly!
With love?
Maybe?
With sex?
Most definitely.

Our Words

Forget the smug fucks
The bubble people
Who live life
Floating over all
Dispensing condescension.
These words are our words,
These are my words,
Words that lurk in shadows,
Words that drift in dreams,
Words that carry joy and sorrow.
Our words embody gold
Sifted from the life we share.
We all know gold when we see it,
It welds us together
By the words we choose to speak.

Letting Go

Just imagine letting go
Of all that unmanageable,
Just lying down
In your life as it has been
As it always will have been
Just exhaling all the pain
All the loss and the joy
Every love every child
Grandchild every friend
Are wholly left to others.
Care entrusted to those who care
To carry the burden
Until they too will reach out
And let go the baton
Letting go has to be
Our last and lasting gift.

The Young Jihadi

He stood knife in hand
The other knelt
They had been through it before
In pretence of execution
Death again anticipated
On this occasion realised
And then the sawing began
For childhood's appalling gift
Ending all innocence.

We are compelled to ask
And did he survive beyond
Whatever we can call
This act beyond belief?
Handing a head to his child?
In some featureless future
Will he remember?
Could he forget?

Will he lose the will to kill?
Will he suppress the memory?
Will it sink into the pit of his life
And become habitual?
We can only hope he bears the cost
One day:
that he smells the blood
That he hears the screams
That he sees the scene mirrored
In his child's eyes forever.

And what about the sin?
Genesis must have it wrong.
How can we speak of a fruit,
a woman, a man and a snake
A trite original sin, when
To reveal the worst that we can be,
We can have a father with a knife
An innocent life
And a child holding a severed head.

What we Know?

Nothing!
We are standing still.
Rubbish!
Our planet is revolving
Travelling through space
Quite quickly.
Do we feel it?
No! We suffer
The existential illusion
The appearance of stability
When everything is in flux.
But we standing in the kitchen
And the dishes need washing
The children need feeding
The future needs imagining
All accepted
For sacred security.

There's Always One

Five galahs gather
Beneath the peach tree
In the orchard
Late afternoon.
They do their thing
They peck at the ground
For a while
And then one,
There's always one,
Wants what another has
And it's on.
Envy the enemy
Is all it takes
To destroy any gathering.

The Pallid Stream

There is a sadness
that sometimes
simply flows through us,
a pallid stream,
moving nothing as it flows,
dissolving the sheen,
leaving a dulled surface,
beyond which nothing shines.
Then as bright
as you might know the world to be,
it appears dull.
The world reflects nothing,
and after a time
the dullness cannot be seen,
and yet it rises in our lives
and determines all that we see
and understand.

Your Path

Let the ancient lines describe
The scattered map left beside
Your path, shattered by stones.

Age and waning strength
Obscure the path you took
From then to now.

Stumbling stubborn rages on
Ignoring wounds and draining strength
With fears and hatreds worn
Let the mountains stop you dead
And let the waters feed you.

And linger long and longer yet
You'll find your map
You'll find your net
And capture all you need to last
Until the end.

It Can Only Be Said

It can only be
It can only be said
In the dark of the night
It can only be seen
When the pin drops unheard
It can only be sensed
In silence with noise
It can only be touched
With a heart broken so
It can only be.

In Ancient Times

In ancient times
When sun bells rang
The wizards leapt
And angels sang
Life was such and much
And ready to the touch
But fragile as it's always been
And what a fuss
Perfumed and restless
At noon and beyond
Circling skywards
Beyond our reach
We were confined
Straightened
And pursued to an end
Often our own
But it was like that then.

Shedding

A snake sheds its skin,
As the detritus falls away
The new is revealed
Shiny, glossy, and smooth.
We can do the same
Not with creams, oils, or unguents
But with insight and design.
We can shed the bitter past
The crass, the desiccated
It can peel away to unveil anew
A skin that better reveals you
Deep, complex, and true.

Storm

The sky blackened
And laden dropped
To the treetops.
There punctured
It set free the flood
In wave upon wave
On helpless earth
With no choice but to weep
New rivers
Sweeping debris away.
The flood also unleashed
Torment on minds
Not cleansed but deafened
By the continuing crash
On tile and tin
Unrelenting day and night
Intense anguish
Until the end.

Not Living

Not living can mean
more than not breathing.
It could be being smothered,
Not by Mother Earth,
But by obsession,
Depression, anxiety.
Not living is everywhere;
We are being infected by the unliving,
The media, the Politicians,
The corporations, the Trumps
The Palmers of this world,
Dysfunctional liars with odiferous breath
Blown into our every orifice.
And the defiling delifers,
We can't forget them
And their deadly ambition
To rid the world of life,
Through various techniques
To bring out the worst in us,
The stuff that directs us
To unlife.

Dawdling Down the Street

Sometimes I dawdle down the street
And am stopped and asked
'What do you think?'
I usually say 'I don't!'
So then I'm told what to think
And it's never nice.
Apparently, I'm supposed to hate
Muslims, refugees, black people
And bankers.
I have no trouble with the latter,
But what have the former ever done
To me or to anyone else?

What is it about these demands to hate?
We hear them all the time
Usually from the bitter and twisted,
Vague and harshly retiring,
Now emboldened by social media,
Revealing their number
And therefore their strength.
They walk down the street,
They go on and on TV,
And they stand in parliament
With a mission to hate, to scar,
A mission to crucify, to destroy.
What is it with them?

On Death in the Orchard

It is fresh
and the sun sets
as always.
The children
next door play happily.
Wattle birds
drive crows away noisily.
None of these know
that it is Anzac Day
A sacred day
for those who share
The shiny gloss of war.

For God's Sake!

As I speak to you,
You who read these lines,
I can, since we have minds,
And language, and names.
We belong in our world,
Each a centre of a universe.
But then there are some of us,
Bombed at home, in school,
In hospitals, with men
Degraded, tortured, murdered,
And boys, girls, women,
Young and old, raped, slaughtered.
Why, for God's sake?
I don't think so.

www.ingramcontent.com/pod-product-compliance
Lightning Source LLC
Chambersburg PA
CBHW062153100526
44589CB00014B/1824